Beyond the Blockade
Seeking Beauty in Melancholy

Beyond the Blockade
Seeking Beauty in Melancholy

KETMANEE

Illustrated by Michael Barr Waltz

nb new ballad

ISBN: 978-1-7357155-9-9 (paperback)
ISBN: 978-1-7357155-8-2 (ebook)

Library of Congress Control Number: 2020948764

First Edition 2021.

Written by Ketmanee.
Illustrated by Michael Barr Waltz.
Book Design & Cover Image by Ketmanee.

New Ballad Publishing
New York

www.newballad.com
www.ketmanee.com

To Me and You and Our Conscience

I. Overture

II. Clavier Sonata

III. Scarlet Suite

IV.   Pathétique Lamentoso

V.   Coda

I. Overture

KETMANEE

My World

Welcome to my world.
I accept the embrace
of opportunity. I fight the time.
From the unspoken silence,
to the running waters
of my tears.

I tear
apart the loneliness of this world
and flood the waters
with my embrace.
"Do not speak in silence,"
they say. "For there is no time."

Your pendulum tells me my time
here is running out. I shed a tear.
I do not speak in silence,
I shout to the world.
Hear me, embrace
my being, drown me in virulent waters.

I feel the warmth of the rainwater
and realise this is the only time
I feel free, for I am suffocated by expectation's embrace.
"No more tears."
I cry. Gravity and love hold the world
together, but not the reluctant silence?

In the comfort of my forgotten silence
I learn to swim mindless waters.
I am reminded that the world's
scarcest resource is time.
It is only now that I notice the tearing
of bonds that hold together beautiful embraces.

To mend the embrace
one must break the silence
by tearing
open the seeds of secrets and watering
them to grow the tree of life. Only time
and self can change the world.

It was *his* embrace that drowned me in water
and held my silence for the last time.
Now, I tear it *all* out of my world.

Power

Elegance, but structure.
They mutter.
For the power
the people?
Let them know.

Gold rests on mahogany silk.
Shine of glory and gore.
The closed toe fades in the darkness.
Collars sharp as blades
drip tears of pearls.
For is it right?
or is it wrong?
For the power
the people?
Rings of banded time, class contradictions
and there is none.

Pinocchio grows his nose here.

Hang Me Up to Dry

I hang up my laundry today. I air it out. I let it dry.
Naked now I am; who needs these coverings when
I have you.
They are just crumpled pieces of my heart.

Burning hatred and loving affection fills my soul.
I've stripped down and
I lay bare.
Can you hear the tiny violin playing the saddest
song for you?
I do.
Because I sing the song.

II. Clavier Sonata

The Phantom

Waking up on your shoulder.
These late-night denials.
Overdue are the party favours.
Unworldly was my adagio.
Haunted by my adolescent specters.
A supernatural sensation.
Susceptible to swallow.

Solo Piano

By the roses, by the thorns.
After what precedent, I leave myself lorn.

.

.

.

Awaiting permission to be indispensable.
Wishing you would let me in.

Ignore everybody else.
Focus on me.

Serenade in Monochrome

Draped by dawn
and its beautiful melody;
We are alone now.

Give me your eyes.
I have yet to decipher this rendition.
These comforting sounds vex my conditioned ears
as the sky dips back to grayscale.

What will it take for you to notice?

The Ivory Chronicles

I loosened the locks.
Peeled back the layers,
and slipped off the pages.

Hoping I was not merely a souvenir,
we vowed to fulfill a bated destiny.

Hold me tight and strengthen your grip.
You were privy to my conspiracy and I cannot undo.

Close to You

When I think of you,
I feel you get closer.

Let's make this real.
You know what happens next.

Come over and stay.
I might just let you fall in love with me.

Hold My Breath

You give me a feeling.
Like saccharine honey in my hands.
Igniting flames in the warm water
as our bodies roam together in the smoldering heat.
Asphyxiate me with your erogenous kisses.
Intoxicated with ecstasy,
I am dripping for your ardent touch.
Yearning for an endless affair.
Your carnal love,
Giving me life.

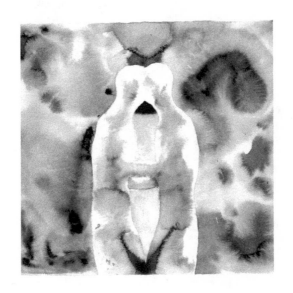

III. Scarlet Suite

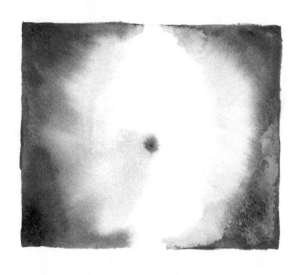

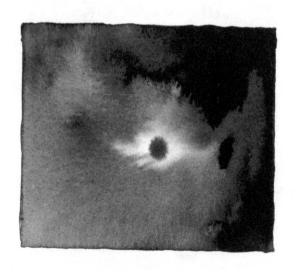

KETMANEE

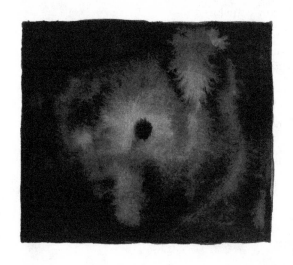

Pleasures of the Flesh

My soul, there is a hunger.
But it is a thirst that I am confused.
Staring at me -- Eight Swords.

Captivated
Magnets we are.
The static so strong,
we must turn humid.

I am exiled and set in a crater.
Insulate my soul
And pleasure my pain.

I want the physical,
I want your lust.
You feel with all your fervor.
Crave me. Desire
Ablaze.

You are one, but not my only.
Love me with your pollution
and I will cure it
with the rain.

A most beautiful poison drowning
my sanity.
Let go of my incandescent anxiety.
Release me.
Restraint.
We can only try.

All consuming --
I want it all consuming.
Come again.
Come again. Come.

And then inevitably,
we are none.

Suffocated by thoughts
of you.

Resist me,
my irresistible.

All of My Time

I have lost myself in my lust for you.
Wanting you.
A waiting game I cannot win
And it is all so tragic.

Hang on, my escape.

Sequel

So pitiful my darling,
Teach me while I unravel my woes that cling
onto you,
to my douleur,
to this forbidden love,
I hope you hear me.

Shall we go again?

The echoes of our muted strings pulsate in my mind.
A cinematic orchestra ever so faint.
I am afraid.
I am afraid
to be afraid.

Abate my cyclone.

My vulnerability casts its shadow and
Black roses melt in the park.

Precious, precious,
No longer
We are.

Isolated Intimacy

Lose yourself and find me.
I hold you tight and you exhale
as the fumes caress our egos.
Masking an image of an ideal I know not.

Thrown back into our stagnant repetition,
We are contaminated.

Let me be well.
Drain me of your venom.
Bleed me. From your ghost.

Fragile -- you know me,
is my soul.
See the glint of the filthy dust
as I let go.

Dopamine

We used to be innocent.

The way you moved,
the way I moved onto you.
My advances welcomed with amorous fumes.
We were acquainted.

Now, the sharp edges of your touch linger,
the sting -- it burns.
My feeble withdrawals cry out my unrequited
heartache.
Self-medicated thoughts to satisfy me.
Feed this toxic blaze and torture me more --
Get me *off* . . . of you.

Dichotomy on dopamine, Rapt.
Addicted in these daydreams.
You have me dazed -- I go numb.

So, tell me your alibi.
I stand stagnant
and you congest me with your chloroform.
Oh, how sweet and still the air,
as it ceases my abstracted euphoria.

Vertigo

Heat wave, heart pounding,
I lose my balance.
Slow motion, my tunnel vision.
Subtle are the stabs.
Freeze frame.
Anamorphic hallucinations of our hyperreality.
Choking on my regurgitation
Till I feel no more.

The sight of your consciousness was my catalyst.
Allergic to the pollen I dismissed.

Viridity

You never mean to -- do you?

Your naïve innocence was a misunderstanding.
A mindless demonstration of our youth
posing with candor like it was an unstained purity.
But really, nothing's true.

Collapse

How do I know if it was true?
Probably when I stop hating you.

Trying to catch a breath but I can't be still.

Every phase ends.
Now slowly,
let me down.

Waning Innocence

We were enshrined in the temples of avidity.
Drifting rogues,
We did it with impunity.

I pray you rewind, relive our gold rendezvous
As there was no infamy.

Because these faltering ultraviolets
are dead cells that flake off my skin.

Titanium cylinders that split,
exploding under my chin.

Where was the line?
Draw it for me.

This is what it feels like.
You will see.

Entangled

Plead for me; I am longing.

We were so painfully intertwined,
Arduously undefined.
You fell in love with the drama but
I just wanted your attention.

I wonder if you still think of me.
Waiting for my atonement.

Violet Trees, Black Skies, &
Nocturnal Animals

Trapped between the starlight.
Projecting vectors
and shooting spirals.

Vibrations dive,
wavelengths collide,
Beyond the blockade.

We came across,
in between,
Mind trips.

Shadows misinterpreted in the night.
You spill me over,
Circle on a line.

. . .

My eyes flooded with feelings of you.
Shaken awake, drowning -- for you.
Breathe me in and I will stay. Give into me.

You knew there was no possibility.
This was a heartbreak of a different kind.
Disintegration loops.

Love, loss --- repeat.

IV. Pathétique Lamentoso

38   KETMANEE

Regality & The Intimate

Better to live without knowing than to live in error.
I live in fantasy.

Nostalgic for the future,
Seeking beauty in melancholy.

Push down on my shoulders.
Why are you so afraid?
of falling short again.

Crucify me.
It is a cold winter.

Extroverted Introspection

See me through the glass ---

opaque.

Shatter me to pieces.

Flip a coin.

Over and under.

Toss me ---

up and down.

Fragile to the sensitivity.

If only that were my weakness.

Tethered

A cerebral insufflation
I surrender.

Grappling with
The emptiness
so I know you care.

[Taut harmonies]

Shackled in a cathartic passion
My bravado.

Fixated on a parallel love.

[Strings swell]

Attention, Madness

Do you see me, or did I run away?
Irresistible and lured to one's destruction,
internal and external --
Send me your tears; I'll dry them.

Did I take my time and wait around? For what,
Motivation from the competition of impression?

Are we clear? Clear we are not,
one of me but really
this is social limitation.

Find direction,
fine my direction.

Desire, do we dare?
Why can't I just need me?

Inspiration and I live,
in this moment -- you are here.

Pre-warranties and priorities; what I am not good at.
I do not know -- I just want completion.

Self-Control

I look at myself and wonder,
Where is my body?
Where is my mind?

Floating in transience.
Still, it feels awfully everlasting.
A perpetual cycle I cannot terminate.

Reel me in,
as I have drifted too far.
Seeking a purposeful intention
from where I have departed
My latent reticence.

My stoicism,
in need of repair.

Blind My Realism

These clouds of rain
blind my realism.

Adrift in identity storms,
Unconscious in this time lapse.

You shattered my façade.

Yet your intimacy
is not intimate,

And time is not a formula.

That turns off the sunset
and cures the darkness
That fails to forget

Me.

The Colours Were So Bright

Faded.

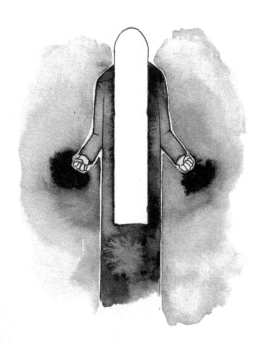

KETMANEE

Noir

Ethereal delusion.
Bleak.

Are my flaws.

Dark is the night with no shadows.
Follow me home where you will not find me.

A psychological tease.
I am.

The nightmare.

I'm dangerous.
But you want it.

Dark Adaptation

Do you dream in colour?

One billion pixels.

Then why are we black and white?

. . .

Blinded by your dim affection.

My eyes turn to night vision.

A darkness so bright and full of vivid crimson.

Odile

Feathers rustle in the restless night.
It is a soulless glamour. Black with no light.
Mystery consumes her.

A mad woman. A bad woman. Guile and slick.

Salacious and vile.

A freak.

A disturbed psychosis.
Blood flows from a twisted delusion.

You know --

I am not,
Not guilty.

Mercy

Girl with the tattoo.
An exotic mysticism.

A lascivious aggression.

Make an exception.

Pull me back to earth.

Make me feel nothing
and run up my mind.

When you come for me.

Siren

Let me see you. Silhouette.
Playing me gently like piano keys so calm and delicate.
My café song. Juxtaposed in my chaotic template.
Manic for my madness. Mellow in my mood.
Read me. Red. Divinity in mind.

The Puppeteer

I am the ringleader.
I pull the strings.

Stroking your ego.
Commanding your concern.
Forcing frustrations on your transformation.

Have no patience for my mind control.
Let me need you.

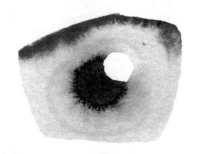

KETMANEE

Pisces Interlude

Meek is the forecast.
Turn me over in the hurricane.

The birthday effect.

Give me a rain jacket for this thunderstorm.
I am waking up down.

Episode 3

Tell me I've lost it.
Tell me it's done.
Tell me I'm nothing.
Tell me you've won.

Tell me you hate me.
Tell me while I cry.
Because you hate that I love you
And you don't know why.

Tell me I'm broken.
Tell me. It's true.
Tell me I've failed you.

Tell me I can't stay.
Tell me I'm not the same.
Tell me I don't care.
When you know we're both in pain.

Tell me it was a sin.
Tell me I'm not your kin.

KETMANEE

Jump Cuts

I watch it take shape.

Savour the good -- toss in the bad.
No verity.

Sometimes I ask myself if it's an illusion . . .

Beautiful madness

Six feet down.

In My Loneliness

In my loneliness, I find you.
I find you in my loneliness.

Nobody wanted your scars.
We do all that is wrong but
We can make it alone -- If we tried.

Tonight, it will be my worst
Because the darkness brings forth its stars.
I have paced around for hours.
Maybe, we will see.

Meltdown

It is the darkest hour.

Permeating through me, this poison.
A carafe of condensed pressure
Cascading instability.

Tinctures of concentrated radiation
Remain from my nuclear decay.

I panic,
Paralysed in my volatile anxiety and
Spiral deeper into my despair.

State of My Fury

It was not my intention.
But the state of my fury has caused more harm
than none.

Aggravated by your vacillation,
I let it consume me.

A feverish rage created by confusion
Exacerbated by uncertainty,
Heightened with insecurity.

Remorseless,
I shed no tears of contrition
As you recoil into your aversion.

Balance to Avoid Sabotage

A cosmic void
Filled with insidious deception.
You have me dancing on a capricious seesaw.

Does my charisma offend you?

My motive, your virtuoso.
We are stars of the same scheme.

I am not the villain.
What's your excuse?

Hubris

What is it we seek?
Power?
Recognition?
What shall be its worth?
Desire has drowned me.

[Awake]

I look in the mirror,
Maybe it was me.
My subconscious conflict and its
Over-indulgent,
Impulsive impurities.

We are stuck in ourselves.
Waiting.
Feigning impressions
Factor into our demise.

Tears flow down my face,
And I wonder
If my mind has gone?
How about my soul?

This life.
This quest.
Tell me, why?
What is it we seek?
Desire has drowned me.

[Asleep]

I am.
In this life.

V. Coda

KETMANEE

In Time

How much longer?
For me to be enough.

Be with.
Grasping the ephemeral.

Time is delicate.
We should not be so rough.

Behaviour Alteration

Hatred,
was what I felt.

I ran from my offenses.
Neglecting morality with little compunction.
Replaying misdemeanors with no punishment.

The erratic fallacies of
one's former egregious state
are admonitions for a future self.

Artifice of the Ego

This cunning arrogance
Gives me a reason to believe
In my own pretention.
A deafening sophistication with no limitation.

This artificial truth is but an imitation.
My savagery, at times gaudy,
Stems from a responsibility
To be somebody.

Infinite

No fear
In Eternity.
Prosperity grows from the pain.
With it,
Freedom to endure.
Freedom to attempt to be whole.
As for love,

I still believe.

Always & Forever

You and me, always.
Our wandering souls.

Stunted by passivity.
We would have been idle.

Forever was not never,
Yet never meant forever.

So, do not turn around.
Eurydice has gone.

My eternal,
I thank you for your affliction.

Anticipating happiness
Is now my pursuit.

Deep Space

Desire has its own rules.
The laws of nature cannot confine.

I am floating out of orbit,
not strapped to your belt.

An alien on other planets.
It has always been me and myself.

Lost in the World

They test me, these emotional flames.
 It hurts although at times I enjoy the pain.

A symphony filled with conflict and confusion.
 It is much to think.

I seek refuge in my dreams
 Leaving ashes in the ink.

Never Let Me Go

Hold on to what's left of me,

I will remain.

Honey Lavender

For what is it we live?
The prospect of life.
The proclivity of one.
We are trespassers.
Mortals of the melancholy
United by symptoms of
Humanness.
I am deserving in
My cultivation of Joy.
The inspiration,
Let it fill me.
The expectation,
Let go of me.
Time does not stand
Yet I will wait.
Nothing scares me anymore.

Afterword

As seen through the lens of a young lover, this
collection visualizes a journey of growth and
maturity while dissecting the dualities of identity,
desire, sexuality, and manifestations of the ego.

The chapter titles, inspired by classical music
nomenclature, serve to underscore and
complement a narrative that,
when presented,
evokes a visceral reaction.

A poetic symphony with an atypical
five movements --
Coda serving not as a finale but
perhaps as a piece to be continued --
I invite the reader to draw upon
their own conclusions.

Beauty is that which needs not an explanation.

About the Author

Ketmanee is an artist and poet based in New York. An old soul, her works in poetry, art direction, film, and installation design encompass philosophies of beauty and human connection while evoking a unique sensuality. She holds a bachelor's degree in International Relations and minors in Music Industry and Cinematic Arts from the University of Southern California.

Ketmanee has produced short films, represented both visual and musical artists in the fine art, singer-songwriter, electronic, and trip-hop realms, and assumed various roles in the arts and media industries as an art advisor, artist manager, PR consultant, and marketer. Her diverse, multidisciplinary background and experiences have shaped her artistic vision, culminating in her aspiration to create meaningful work that connects both the rational and the emotional.

Beyond the Blockade is Ketmanee's debut poetry collection.

CPSIA information can be obtained
at www.ICGtesting.com
Printed in the USA
BVHW071043150221
600147BV00003B/332